CLUSTERS

CLUSTERS

poems by
Kenneth Sherman

*For Ken,
who helped in my
conversations with the Muse.*

Ken/97

Mosaic Press
Oakville, ON. - Buffalo, N.Y.

Canadian Cataloguing in Publication Data

Sherman, Kenneth, 1950-
Clusters

Poems.
ISBN 0-88962-638-3
I. Title.
PS8587.H3863C58 1997   C811'.54   C97-930018-5
PR9199.3.S53C58 1997

No part of this book may be reproduced or transmitted in any form, by any means, electronic or mechanical, including photocopying and recording information storage and retrieval systems, without permission in writing from the publisher, except by a reviewer who may quote brief passages in a review.

Published by MOSAIC PRESS, P.O. Box 1032, Oakville, Ontario, L6J 5E9, Canada. Offices and warehouse at 1252 Speers Road, Units #1&2, Oakville, Ontario, L6L 5N9, Canada and Mosaic Press, 85 River Rock Drive, Suite 202, Buffalo, N.Y., 14207, USA.

MOSAIC PRESS, in Canada:	MOSAIC PRESS, in the USA:
1252 Speers Road, Units #1&2,	85 River Rock Drive, Suite 202,
Oakville, Ontario, L6L 5N9	Buffalo, N.Y., 14207
Phone / Fax: (905) 825-2130	Phone / Fax: 1-800-387-8992
E-mail:	E-mail:
cp507@freenet.toronto.on.ca	cp507@freenet.toronto.on.ca

MOSAIC PRESS in the UK and Europe:
DRAKE INTERNATIONAL SERVICES
Market House, Market Place,
Deddington, Oxford. OX15 OSF

Mosaic Press acknowledges the assistance of the Canada Council, the Ontario Arts Council and the Dept. of Canadian Heritage, Government of Canada, for their support of our publishing programme.

Copyright © Kenneth Sherman, 1997
ISBN 0-88962-638-3
Cover and book design by: Susan Parker
Printed and bound in Canada

CONTENTS

I	The Public Pier	11
	Huckleberry	12
	Prints	13
	Playing Baseball With My Son	14
	Sailor's Ear	16
	Spray	18
	Florida	19
	Summer Camp	20
	The Suburbs	21
	The Wheel	23
	Man And Wave	24
	Landscape	
II	Clusters	29
III	The Galapagos Tortoises	43
	In Memoriam: Adele Wiseman	46
	Gwen	48
	Mahabalipuram	50
	Pondicherry, 1973	52
	Achziv, 1969	53
IV	Presence	57
	Notes	58
	Jumbo	59
	Love Objects	60
	Psalm	62
	The Sabbath	63
	Gaberdine	64
	The Gulf	66
	This Nation	67
	The Cold	68
	Janus	70
	Winter Fishing	71
	Cross-Country	72
	North	73
	Narrow Road	74
	Night Music	75

Acknowledgments

ARC, Cross Currents (U.S.), *Descant, Midstream* (U.S.), *Poetry Canada Review, Prairie Fire, Queen's Quarterly, The New Quarterly, Viewpoints.* ''North,'' and ''Sailor's Ear'' first appeared in the anthology *Borderlines* (Copp Clark, 1995).

flashes of consciousness in the oblivion of days

Mandelstam

by the same author

poetry

Snake Music
The Cost of Living
Words For Elephant Man
Black Flamingo
Relations (editor)
The Book of Salt
Jackson's Point
Open to Currents

prose

Void and Voice

I

THE PUBLIC PIER

I remember its blond planks
and the initials of lovers
carved with penknife
or burned with a magnifying glass
that had focussed the sun. Hearts,
dates, proclamations of affection
whose endurance no one could guess.
It was held up by a primal crib:
algae-covered timber and boulders
where my feet slipped, where I'd dive
to find blurred bottles, fish hooks,
lost sinkers, lures, and disconnected lines.
Last year I returned to find it gone,
a blue vacancy, a gross and gaping space
that shocked like an amputation,
a confirmation that my friends
doing cannonballs off the edge
to startle the older girls sunbathing
(so mysterious in their dark sunglasses),
anglers, elderly card players, panting dogs,
and ice-cream licking toddlers in strollers
(their young mothers swaying
to static-riddled love songs
from the transistor radios)
were all only sunlit ghosts
breathing in my head.
All things under the sun perish
but under the surface -
broken claws of the crayfish,
the great, moping bass.

HUCKLEBERRY

Aged seven,
I lay in bed with a fever
read to by Mrs. Rowlands, our neighbour,
her voice of seventy years
speaking Huck's green grammar
leading me to the heart's frontier...

My life of longings, escapes.
The continents I've covered,
the million-odd eyes
that have brushed against mine.
Now I know:
that slave I worked to set free
is me - my raft
this tenuous craft
carrying me through currents of darkness
to where the ghosts grieve
because they are misunderstood.
There I see myself,
a runaway boy in the narrow ravine,
walking by the creek
that is forever too shallow,
making my impossible plans.
Attentive to the shrieking birds,
the flying shadows,
I have already entered
into my deep exile
where the trees seem to breathe
and bend
toward a word.

PRINTS

Above my childhood headboard
were prints of galloping cowboys,
frontiersmen. Some of the faces
were clean-shaven, rugged Midwest,

others - drooping blond moustaches
and wind swept brims
above the pillow where I dreamt
of six-shooters, spurs, a ten gallon hat.

The unpredictable zigzag of sagebrush.
An insolent cloud of dust.
And what was my wish? To be gone
from unpromising pavement

into a horizon unknown, without limits,
where presence is only suggested
by smoke signals, trails, a solitary
set of hoof prints centering the vast expanse.

PLAYING BASEBALL WITH MY SON

It is more than a sphere of stitched leather
that is passed between the generations
in slow parabola or thrown hard
because a father's love
should sometimes sting the hand.

It takes me back
to weeds in centre field,
the deep lull of a June afternoon
when all things were possible
and I imagined myself to be Mantle.

Icons fed the mythical:
sportscards, record books,
stats of earned-run averages,
lineups of the great
and what they said

all kept in the gum-sweetened darkness
of my boyhood dresser.
I seem to have traded all that
for this mantle of language.
Still, I love the contact:

smack of the ball on leather,
crack of the bat,
drama of an arm outstretched -
the perfectly pocketed
white period

that you hold now,
the tangible confidence
that comes with its weight,
its hardness. It is
a small planet

that you've learned
to make live with curves
and change-ups, those unexpected
shifts that somehow resemble
a life's discontinuous events.

Who knows what fate
will throw us? But this will keep,
burned deep into love's pocket:
the June sun, the diamond,
the white, anchored bases.

SAILOR'S EAR

What had us out those early mornings,
me with pen and paper,
you the boy discoverer combing the shore
for seashells, free treasure?
Smooth spirals, ridged fans.
The tiny ones dropped into a jar of winter sun.
Go ahead, wash and label them.
They have names to look up in a book
like *flamingo tongue, sailor's ear*,
and the three-inch *lettered Venus* -
so much desire in the language you'd think
they'd been invented by anonymous poets,
dreaming seafarers. And my fear
is that our fluid morning hours together
will be reduced to just a photograph
of me in a bleached-out beach chair,
my pen momentarily lifted from the pad,
you in the foreground squinting for the snap
raising your sea-pink trophy
for the instantaneous lens,
the two of us caught in the framed imitation -
so static. What then would I wish?
That in the years to come
when you press this fighting conch
to your ear you hear no duplication,
no dreary note of eternity
but a voice that incites beginnings,
those possibilities that lead to the actual
and what you gathered in your bright pail:

the primal crimsons, cool, crustaceous,
the bivalves' cloud-like swirls of grey,
and their names
sounding our unknowable depths.

SPRAY

Each summer he wonders
if he still has what it takes.
A sudden argument
from the engine and he is yanked
out of the cold cradle of the lake,
his vision blurred
by the wall of white water.
He claims his balance,
adjusts his weight,
cuts hard across the green surface
sending a shiver of spray.
Not as deep or as close
as he did in his youth,
but close enough to know
some vestige of his former self
exists, for there's that shadow
speeding alongside of him,
unaged, dark
and featureless.

FLORIDA

Stevens thought it a "palmy beach"
extending as far as the mind's horizon.
At night, the wind off the genital sea
spoke of a state of becoming, while for Hemingway
the Keys were outposts where the hard-edged
stared into the uncompromising abyss.
Ms. Bishop thought it a chorus-line of fragrant words:
flamingo, mangrove, tanager - and a galaxy of shells:
the Ponderous Ark, Wings of Angel - the Coral Alphabet.
For those who arrive with all that luggage
there are the malls, the gold-painted pineapples,
the banal blue pools to get through
and the Parks whose theme is disappointment.
From Canaveral to Key Largo the coastline flows
with a ceaseless traffic which sounds like waves.
At night, it is lit by miles of neon advertising chains.
To break free you must go down to the darkened beach
and watch the surf flash like phosphorous
or travel to the old inland waters, still, reflective,
where everything has stopped and the swamp remembers.
The moon shines like the lost breastplate of Ponce de Leon
and the humid wind carries the ghostly voices
of Seminole Indians.
In that web of vegetation
you will hear your own breath, you will hear
the sudden splash of the alligator submerge,
his tail punctuating the silence.
SUMMER CAMP

SUMMER CAMP

Our little ones are gone.
Now our most important person
seems to be the mailman
who brings their sometime letters
with the address slanted upward -
their fledgling selves transmitted
through the hastily, pencilled script.

We read and grasp at morsels,
hunger for more details.
But already part of them is private.
They grow away from us
and close with a string of X's,
a trail
of diminishing kisses.

THE SUBURBS

I too dislike the scenery:
the uninspired lawns,
the freshly sealed driveways,
the predictable turn of sprinklers.
Those who live with abundance
yet somehow wish for more.

Who can plumb the contradictory depth
of that hunger
and that uneventful ordinariness
that's become an easy target
for both the social worker
and the poet?

For something in us wants this:
a place to be unafraid
and generally unnoticed;
to be quietly productive,
unwilling to admit how prosperity
permits us to live and let live.

It is true. There are painful regrets
and dramas behind each door,
days we would rather forget.
But how considerate the region is
with its regular
goings and comings. Its appearances.

Whatever it is we've surrendered
is sensed in the evening
as we watch the darting birds
cut through thickening dusk
and know that something
larger, something secretive

is held constrained under
the asphalt and pavement. We ask
if there were once gods in the cedars
who have abandoned us. We wonder,
as night wraps around like a mask,
at the pressing disorder of stars.

THE WHEEL

You're alone amongst buoyant pairs -
those couples whose hands are entwined
as the tilting carriages climb
the windless summer air.

When it stops at the top, you totter.
Relax. Enjoy the view. The fits
and screams from those on The Vortex
are muffled, as if underwater.

All things below seem true:
The strollers, the tents,
the balloons, the pennants,
and off to the left, over blue,

sea gulls that glide to their food,
boats that course in silence
with a force you hardly notice,
perched at this altitude.

In a moment you'll start to come down.
See that man who handles the lever:
Gruff stubble and serpentine hair,
eyes hardened by counting the rounds.

What a radical change in perspective
now that you've coldly come eye-level
with his bulging tattoo of a devil
and a sign that says, Watch Your Step.

MAN AND WAVE

So he heard it,
a sibilance rushing the shore,
the drawn-out breathing
of a cosmic sleeper,
lost lullaby heard first in childhood
and before that
the rhythm of maternal blood
echoing through the expectant fluid.
Alien now, he tried to figure what it said.

He walked closer, listening
as if the mystery might be solved
but like suds from a washer
the surf dissolved in the sand
leaving only the bare-chested conundrum
of a man in a swimsuit
freely entering the element
the crest of his self rising
to meet the wave coming in.

LANDSCAPE

In the end, the only country left to
face is the one each has founded:
no hand on the heart, no flag, no anthem.

The sound that a rock makes
when it is rushed at by wind.

II

Look at the flowers, so faithful to what is earthly,
to whom we lend fate from the very border of fate.
And if they are sad about how they must wither and die,
perhaps it is our vocation to be their regret.

-- Rilke

CLUSTERS

1
What will open and close: doors,
days, eyes, valves, and ventricles.

A canticle then for the impermanent
and what will be repeated.

2
Spring, the predictable and potential.
There was possible blockage:
the brown insulation of leaves,
bleached newspaper trapped all winter,
early weeds. I raked that clear.
Still there were the clods and pebbles
to break through. Seen from the shoots' perspective -
planets, boulders.
But now they're here,
a row of underworld couriers,
your grape hyacinths -
                      delectable clusters.

3
What comes first
should be miraculous.
But I am oddly detached
like the rest of this garden,
still stunned by winter
and by your leaving-
a spectator
of these minuscule bells.

4
Your pale hands planted them,
reaching down into that region
devoid of clouds and angels.
Density of roots, minerals and the strange
meeting of the sixth finger -
thick earthworm, our future worker.

All our years together:
but who are you with your clear eyes?
We were two types: what I saw into,
you saw through. A wind comes up.
There are no leaves yet to rustle.
And your image fluctuates,
is hard to hold onto.

5
And I wonder if it is too late
to define what came between us?
We lived so many years
without drinking these colours,
consumed with concerns, disappointments,
not enough risks ("too many!" you'd say),
not enough tenderness.

I understand your wish to go
once the planting was finished,
but yesterday, while cutting the grass,
I bent to lift a piece of eggshell
on my fingertip,
jagged bit of world,
and wondered if its inhabitant
survived the breakage.

6
The fence has all but vanished.
No one has bothered to raise another
as if neighbours had given up on borders -
a new phase in human evolution.
Why hadn't that seeped into our arguments?
What came between us was a material invisible
yet strict like metal.

Wood chips of posts fifty years old
feed all this struggling green
that will make its appearance
in your absence.

7
Is this then our lives, this
charted lot, this set survey?
Who will talk of the small striving,
fears, watering, the shears I sharpened
("What's cut grows stronger,
but if you cut too much...").
All we can count on are the flowers,
evidence of the kaleidoscopic revolution
from now till autumn,
while we stay the same shade
moving ourselves closer to shades.

8
Was it predictable or strange
that after all those years we still
wondered why the lilac failed to bloom,
whether the juniper was better suited
to the front yard,
asking Mrs. Wilson, our neighbour specialist
for more tips. Her garden, with modest fountain
and butterfly bush, perfect, calm,
though since her husband's death
she's out so seldom.

9
His elaborate feeding system:
the birdhouse he built - tubes, funnels.
In winter, I stood amazed at our back window,
watching, one year after his death,
the burning blues and reds flit against snow -
as if they were messengers
from the speechless region.

10
You were good at growing things.
I watched you kneeling with your work-gloves,
trowel, straw hat. You always kept
a quiet distance between yourself
and existence. A form of respect.
I sometimes barge through things,
damaging incipient bulbs
while eradicating weeds.

You taught me care
and now I stand here alone
watching an indecisive bee zigzag
and hover.

11
Perhaps Voltaire was correct -
to cultivate this small tract
is the place to arrive. But then again,
he lived so much in his head.

Still, when you cross an ocean
you're only invading someone else's garden.
Stay, and it becomes your own.

12
And I liked to travel. Once I incited you
to trek across two continents:
temples, sacred rivers, and most persistently -
ruins. My attraction to what is lost, broken,
yours to what is starting up, settling in:
the cup of light, the reflective carpet,
the hand-warmed banister.
While you were arriving, I was leaving,
but now it's you who's taken the major leap.
Perhaps there's a mathematical proposition
to define our states, like lines that won't converge.
Remember leaving Bombay,
and the sharp geometry of train tracks
that consumed the distance?

13
Difficult to know where things end, begin,
and even these words, perhaps an evasion.
But once you said you heard whispering
beneath the level of your deepest digging.
Out of the fragrant darkness,
the hyacinth, with its blood droplets,
ghost breath calling out
from the quietude of your life
to the stirred region, imploring you
to make up for what you had not lived.

14
To dream out of this and go back years
to when I'd write upstairs
looking out the window at the spray of colours
as you filled our daughter's turtle pool.
Her white sun bonnet, small sail
of memory. So long as things were growing,
you were content. Now it's as if
the goddess of fresh starts
had left this garden still growing
but barren.

15
The children encouraged us to plant
what we never thought of: pumpkins,
sunflowers, fiddleheads -
exotic green harps you said you'd play.
Now they're grown and gone
but the space they left-
a no-man's-land across which our words
sputtered like flares
lighting up the injured.

16
And was it "things" that came between us?
Not grief but the scorecard of grievances:
workload, balances, another love interest,
or those vestiges of parents we thought
we'd talked to rocky death,
or perhaps just tedium - no longer in awe
of our own blooming selves.

Uncontrollable forces
like heat waves, dry wind,
sudden hail - unaccountable.
My terrible ego.

17
"A little bit at a time," Mr. Wilson would say,
and his wife would nod.
They never seemed to exert themselves,
yet not a weed. Even the peas
perfectly creeping up their posted screen.
Strange though, he died on a journey,
the retired homebody out at sea at 84.
Where was the cruise ship?
Far south of the equator.
Perhaps the air was too strange,
the light unfamiliar?

18
You gone too, but not like that,
not food for the roots of your hyacinths,
just breathing different air, greeting
different neighbours - an elemental difference.
Sometimes, I swear I feel your fingers
in the crusted fingers of your work-gloves.

19
The bearded gardener you liked to joke with
who sells manure and fiery petunias
at the Fairlawn Market, asked after you.
I said you had other things to do.
Was I deceiving him, or me?

20
And life, which once seemed so vast,
is small like this garden,
like the white ribbon on your straw hat
I discovered in the basement cedar chest.
Straw's no conductor
but its strands carried me back through our years.
I sat a long time after finding it,
the silence in that underground room, enormous.

21
All of this, a backward glance.
Have I lost you then, to the darkness of separation?
Those gnawing beasts - regret and self-accusation -
(not having said enough, or too much)
calmed for a time by language.

At night they start up
with narrowing eyes
as if deaf to the songs tossed down
to quell their hunger.

In an engraving
one might see them stupefied
with poetry, peering from behind
the trees of an earlier century.

22
It is summer and the purple of your hyacinths
has evaporated.
Small stalks,
spiky, unspectacular.

23
Our moments are ours.
Flowers return here or to some other garden
with the tedium of the eternal
but what was said between us,
distinct, particular,
binds us to passing flesh.
Tell me, where you are,
is there the smell of darkness,
thick clots of rain soaked loam,
the dense congregation of flowers
drugging the summer air?

24
And things feel incomplete.
It is like a late conversation
broken off in mid-sentence
while some winged thing insists
against the midnight screen.

I keep expecting you to call to me
from our kitchen window but when I turn
there is only the shade of the tree,
a vacant picnic table, July's
heartless doldrums. And now
we have all this finishing to begin.

III

THE GALAPAGOS TORTOISES

With their beaked noses,
their weak chins,
their dull, slow-blinking eyes -
who can love them?

They spend their days
in a pilgrimage for water
which in these lava-crusted
islands, is rare.

Remote, plodding,
they may live two hundred years.
Some must harbour memories
of the cursing sailors

who packed their ancestors
in the dark and humid holds
to serve as fresh food stuff -
the green and glittering cargo,

or recall the thirsting Bishop
who toured the sharp cliffs
as well as Darwin with his notepad
mapping Science's abyss.

Faith? Their carapaces
are dusty, flaking.
When they discover water
"they dive as if dying

of thirst.'' Trekking
under the unremitting sun
amongst sparse vegetation,
they carry a quarter-ton

of their labouring selves
in search of the edible.
And how they vanish -
their eggs, grand ovals

ravaged by goats
and wild dogs brought
in bright ships
and left without thought.

Consider Lonesome George,
sole surviving remnant
of the sub-species Pinta,
recently held hostage

by disgruntled fishermen
quarrelling with the government:
posed, on the verge of extinction -
an unphotogenic news item.

Yet rather than pity, we despise them
for being vulnerable,
so slow and unchallenging,
so compliant to our will,

for bearing long witness
to our dark repetitiveness.
We collect their blood in vials
to feed our dreams of Eros,

their oil to bolster
the hopes of the incurable.
We shatter their shells
to manufacture baubles.

I have heard that on the island
deemed most populous
the sound of their mating
is like a drawn-out, eerie chorus

a hundred moaning voices
that break quadraphonic
across the landscape of craters
and lava rocks.

I would like to travel
to that desolate lunar island
and hear for myself
passion mixed with lamentation,

a sound that asks only
its mere continuation,
even there, amongst cacti,
where chances are slim.

IN MEMORIAM: ADELE WISEMAN

1973. Graduate studies.
Drafts of reviews,
fragments of attempted poetry
scattered on my kitchen table.

I spent days that spring
cracking the code of your novel,
deciphering Danile, the father loving
but blind,

his estranged daughter
charged with experience:
that heart-rending narrative
which brought a redemptive myth

to the cold streets of Winnipeg,
reprieving the darkness
with shards of light
that we too were cast in

the first time we met
under the sun-splintered shade
of towering maples
on Bernice Lever's backyard patio.

When I raised the penury of the artist
as if it were some holy banner,
you, pragmatic, countered
with the Chinese injunction:

"Eat first - poetry second."
In profile, physique
and close-cropped hair
I likened you then to Gertrude Stein

for I was reading correspondents
into every tone and gesture,
preparing myself
for a life on the line.

GWEN

Above my writing desk,
a postcard you sent:
One of Utamaro's courtesans
with pale, powdered face,
eyes like sidewise teardrops,
hands clasped in devotion
or enthusiasm, it's hard
to tell which though it's something
positive, as was your message ending

>   "Good Luck,
>   Gwen"

In the cavernous auditorium
reciting like a Russian
(all your lines from memory)
you moved my students
as you focussed on the back doors
and the coal-red letters - EXIT.

The last time I saw you,
by *Future's Bakery*
your round face was pale,
haunted like your moon,
dark armies swarming
in the Sea of Discontent.

It was a face
which had seen its own death,
seen it through eyes,
clear, blue,
luminous.

MAHABALIPURAM

Rock shrines, stone carvings, south of Madras, dating back to 600 A.D.

1

The monkey man.
The bare-breasted lovers
riding through air.

A goddess,
coils of the cobra
from the waist down

all caught
in a state of becoming,
their fluidity frozen

they no longer suffer,
acting the warrior, the fool,
the human animal.

In stone
they have been rescued
from the monotonous groan of ocean

and from the interminable cycle
of darkness
and light.

2

In the temple cave
an enormous stone phallus
and a small bas-relief
of the four-armed god, one hand
cupped about his wife's breast.

But we are restless flesh,
not stone. It is always
twilight in the temple.
Through the entranceway
I see the sun-lit beach, blue sea,
brilliant-coloured saris:
the world of energy and waste
which this silence nourishes.

I touch the humid stone
and its coolness opens a space in me
where the darkness collects.
Light sings beyond the cave
and I move to touch it.

PONDICHERRY, 1973

Then everyone travelled. Longhairs with backpacks
trekking across the poorer continents.
We came upon this morsel of France:
a miniature Arc de Triomphe, restaurants
with calligraphic menus -
totems to soothe the Western eye.
And to rub the Brits, a statue of Gandhi
caught in mid-stride, bare
but for loin-cloth and walking stick -
the sinewy thinness of the political spinner.
His shaved head seemed determined to take on
a large future. Ours was smaller:
frayed jeans and the soft ribs of sandals,
the drained eye of the spectator.

ACHZIV, 1969

I arrived late so I could only hear the sea,
not see it. Moonlight stretched like a carpet
across the heaving darkness, night air burned
with the persistence of salt. Ruins for a hotel ....
Over sleeping bodies, I shone a flashlight
on the wall and saw a faded fresco:
a sea of blue scrolls and ships
and two young men, their mocha faces
flaking into nothingness.
Morning, I met my fellow guests -
Israeli soldiers on temporary leave
and shared the army coffee they called *mud*.
It was dark, like their young eyes and faces
which no one yet had painted.

IV

PRESENCE

Night sky, scent of the staring
blackberries, and your voice
breaking as from a dream
over the lake's slow lapping
against rock. To be here
at this moment
at the centre of a stillness
that defies all forms changing,
ourselves, passing.

NOTES

Your fingerprints on the pillow
won't tell who you are.

All your positions in sleep
will be lost
like indentations in sand.

Your dream
breaks from this room, this street.
No one pursues it.

The clang of the streetcar
and its cargo of ghosts -
shift work of the moon.

The tide of darkness
has washed yesterday from your lips.

Who are you
body breathing in sleep,
notes to be written?

JUMBO

The quiet house.
The great grey elephant of days.

Much going, much coming
but here
in the centre of a slow and curious eye

the broad sweep of a tail
and like a Sting Ray
the great undulating ear.

What I hear when I turn
this page
is the suggestion of wind.

What I take in
is dark and indelible.

LOVE OBJECTS

Door

Your exit, your entrance,
your absence, your presence.
In between, memory
in the singing hinge.

Bed

The turbulence of lovemaking, dreams,
leaves no imprint.
In the morning, made, speechless.
Four legs. The weight
of secrets.

Window

What one sees into
another sees through. Generous
glass.

Lamp

On: the eye of explanation.
Off: lost in an ocean of inwardness.
A quiet click.

Mirror

We are in it.
Perishable portrait.
A surface run over by whispers,
in darkness.

Closet

Clothes dream of bodies.
Hangers collect a veil
of dust. The used, the anticipated.
The reflection of shoes.

Window Screen

Mesh separating us from *it*.
But lets in night's thick lilac.

Tape Deck

Loop of longing.
Two speakers fed by dark wire.
A voice, decades gone,
still hungers.

PSALM

I had become a disbeliever.
But lying here, drawn into your eyes
where the heart is a well-thumbed
prayer book filled with life's many
tears, its few hallelujahs,
I reclaim that boy who stood
wide-eyed before candles and miracles.

If there is you, if there is your breath,
how can there be no spirit, no presence?
I have let the philosopher's stone
fall from my pocket. Better to watch green things
search for light, roots search in darkness
for what only the darkness gives.

And each chaotic life is the commentary
one reads in the margins of a text
which has been titled, Should-Have-Been.
We go on annotating
until the end of our days.

Who made the wastelands, the vast
No? Only we, dark inventors,
walking through canyons of city towers
and by waters which we have poisoned. To love the earth.
To begin, as Adam, gazing into a woman's eyes
which were transformed from a bone,
from bare whiteness. To have words for her
that have their seed
in silence.

THE SABBATH

Many hearts and pitchers are broken at the fountain of profit.

Heschel

Released from the tyranny of things
We are given this day to behold a mystery -
To ask not "How much can be done?"
But "What can be undone?"
A day to enter the temple within,
A day of reversal, when
Far from machinery's making,
The self-judgment that seems unending
("Am I rich, poor, success or failure?")
We walk unencumbered
Through a landscape golden and suspended
Connected to the not-yet-born and the dead,
And stand before Time's awesomeness
Which transforms our pettiness
So we feel compassion for all struggling creation,
Aware that, whether the golden landscape is illusion
Or not, breath is a gift.

GABERDINE

(for Shel Krakofsky)

Sabbath-breaker, I pass them in my car
as they walk beneath a sweet suburban sun.
Aside from storefront English
one might think that this is Lublin,
circa 1936, before the grave events
burned in us those questions
that seem to make their dress irrelevant:

the aristocrat's fur hat
proclaiming man-in-God is noble,
the earlocks reaching out
like a stem's searching tendril,
knee-high, page-white stockings
and the shining gaberdine -
deep beyond the darkest ink.

There is that student in the tale,
the one desiring grace,
who sought his Master not for Torah
but to watch him tie his shoelace!
Gesture. Nuance. Revelation
in the movement of a hand.
Layers in the simplest narrative.

That world has vanished,
and these, the remnant,
anachronistic yet ecstatic,
carry the word upon their lips
while we who have been given
the illusion of direction
stay lost in the flow of traffic.

THE GULF

- *after Baudelaire*

Pascal had his gulf, moving with him when he moved.
Alas - all is abyss: action, dreams, desires,
even language. And oftentimes I feel the flapping wings
of terror stream close above my head.

All around me the deep descending shore,
the air of silence and frightful, enchanting space.
Each night I watch God's finger trace
a multitude of forms, like an unending nightmare.

Sleep frightens like a hole
leading who knows where.
All windows open up into infinity.

I suffer from vertigo,
and long for the insensibility of extinction.
Ah, never to be free of numbers, of Being.

THIS NATION

So many roads, so many spaces.
And the distance between each city
like the darkness between the stars.
And each of us a space traveler

without a map. Oh, they had a plan
those sideburns - their legislature of dollars
and bottled Scotch, a nation linked
by nothing more solid than tracks.

As for dreams, they're
there to read in the spaces,
or in our words which fall
from a winter sky, like stars, unnoticed.

THE COLD

In this country
the cold drives people inside.
Their houses swallow them.
The furnace churns
and they sit in the warm belly
of the great house bear,
filled with a private odor.
When they venture out
they wear hats
or ear muffs and resemble
ridiculous animals.
They flap their arms to keep warm
like people-sized birds.

In summer they emerge
but you can see the winter
has not left them. You see it
in their faces, their movements,
in the way they greet one another,
tentatively, as if there may not be
another summer and winter will last and last
like a condition that is chronic.

But they don't walk to the clinic.
They accept it
the way their ancestors once accepted God -
without singing, without celebration

and in August, in the wilderness,
they stare in amazement
at the profusion of green
and accept the naked silence as a hymn.

JANUS

Toboggans. Ice-rinks. A snowman
with eyes of navy blue buttons,
the inevitable carrot nose.
Everyone then was a sculptor.
The cold shrunk space and the voices
of neighbours drew near.
Inside an icicle, daylight suspended,
its mineral taste
dissolving on my tongue.
There were small ghosts I controlled
with my breath and later,
inside, I curled on the sofa
above the ember-red carpet -
the insistent whirr and generosity
of the furnace.
Through windowpanes
I'd watch the day dissolve
into diminishing greys
and hear the solitary scrape
of a shovel
as darkness settled on those mounds,
on those soft accumulations
building, perishable.

WINTER FISHING

A hole in the ice in our heated makeshift.
The amber bottle set on a barrel.
And he was pouring it out - I mean tales
one more discreditable than the next

shifting from town rumour to major politics:
histories, grief, the net of self-mocking laughter
while outside the wind sounded out
the miles of lake gone desert.

Against that rawness his voice was a comfort
as we sat blinking over dark punctures,
visualizing the slow torpedo of scales,
the locked eyes in the depths below us

suspended between what is cold and colder.
When he stopped talking the wind came in,
the minutes became hours as nothing took hold
and our lines seemed connected to air.

CROSS-COUNTRY

A cold sun is breaking through branches,
dispensing long shadows.

I breathe out embryos of ghosts
that briefly billow, dissolve

as I stride past sentinel lines
of trees without leaves,

the sound of my skis slurring
the stillness of the forest.

I am making tracks,
double impressions indent the whiteness.

The points of my poles leave a script
which will follow me into the distance.

NORTH

If I do not touch this space each year
I feel incomplete,
all my summers connecting
like a canoe's receding wake.

The first dip of the paddle
tests the strong arm of the lake
then in tandem
we are cutting the surface

listening inside to the underside,
to that time before time
when the ear was tuned to the exclamation
of a sudden splash.

When lakes do not connect we make
our awkward portage. The canoe over my head
is the monster beak of a bird
watering the seed of legend.

Something in us still loves God
for we could end all of this.
Our small fires and embers
are mere dots left on a distance

which we've permitted to live
knowing that we require the moss, the rock,
the lake's cold memory of the glacier,
the inarticulate other.

NARROW ROAD

The stillness of January
broken only by bird's wings
breaking free from fir branches.
Temperature below freezing

but sun so intense
you can sit on the porch, coatless,
reading poems
or writing letters owed to friends

in far off countries.
I set down sparse lines
while water drips
from the faucet of hanging ice

thinking of Basho on the north's
narrow road, the ghost breath
of the traveller whose shadow
figures against the snow.

NIGHT MUSIC

A rock is compressed silence.
And water lapping rock is sound
striving to free the deepest ore.
In the interior of night
the loon's call,
the seed of all utterance,
loops back upon itself
after piercing
the vacant darkness.
Where are you?
In the small wake of the water spider?
In the gelid eye of the fish
staring into the well
of its own muteness?
Loneliness not only takes, but feeds
so I go on listening into the spell of night
with its private rustling,
its wooded parenthesis
where a falling branch or star
resonates along the silent spine,
under the sky's stone eye,
blind, but touched
by the source of light.

- Cap-Saint-Ignace
- Sainte-Marie (Beauce)
Québec, Canada
1997